TOM HENRICKSEN

Write Some Code with HTML, CSS, + JavaScript

Contents

Preface

As a developer, I thought I knew enough of HTML and CSS. I was wrong. I had to come back to the basics again and again. That is why I put this together. Plus I feel like JavaScript should be here too.

First, we start with some basics of HTML. You may have seen some of this before, but I find a review helpful. Then we cover some HTML5 changes. We touch on some of the major changes. Then we wrap up HTML with a discussion of tables, divs, and spans. These have confused me more than once...

The second section is devoted to CSS. This helps class things up a bit. We cover CSS basics, the box model, and CSS3. Similar to HTML5 it has some interesting updates.

The third part focuses on JavaScript basics. Covering topics like variables, functions, and conditionals. We also cover loops and closures too. In this quick start guide, we just focus on what you need to start working.

I

HTML

In part one, we start with the basics of HTML. We review the basics of HTML, HTML5, and divs and spans.

1

Targeted HTML Basics For Reliable People

Photo by Jackson Sophat on Unsplash

The web is created with some foundational technologies. Every website uses HTML or Hypertext Markup Language. It makes the content we consume online.

HTML

It gives structure to the pages we see. We can add images and links to a website with a series of elements and tags. Let's look at a simple example to get started.

```
<!DOCTYPE html>
<html>
<body>

<h1>Heading</h1>
<p>Paragraph.</p>

</body>
</html>
```

We start with the DOCTYPE to declare this is HTML. Then we have the open tag for HTML. As you look at the bottom you see the closing tag for HTML too. The body has similar tags to open and close the element.

Heading

We have a heading in our previous example. HTML Headings can be from <h1> to <h6>. It starts large and gets smaller as the number gets bigger.

```
<h1>Heading</h1>
<h2>Heading</h2>
<h3>Heading</h3>
<h4>Heading</h4>
<h5>Heading</h5>
<h6>Heading</h6>
```

If we open this in Chrome this is what you will see.

Heading

Heading

Heading

Heading

Heading

Heading

Heading Example
6

Paragraph

You can use the HTML paragraphs tag when you have a text block. We saw that in our first example. Here is another one.

```
<p>Lorem ipsum dolor sit amet, consectetur adipiscing
elit,
sed do eiusmod tempor incididunt ut labore et dolore
magna aliqua.</p>
```

Now these two are nice elements but the reason the web is powerful is links. Let's look at those next.

Link

The Hyperlink or link in HTML is the secret sauce. We can link to the document source or a reference.

```
<a href="https://codeiseasy.co">Code Is Easy</a>
```

Of course, sometimes we like to see a picture or image on the screen. To do this we need the image tag.

Image

The image tag helps us add visual components along with the text.

```
<img src="tom.jpg" alt="Tom Headshot" width="100"
height="150">
```

I added the width and height but these are not required. Although, it can help to keep the sizing correct.

Lists

HTML gives us two options for lists. Ordered and unordered lists.

```
<h2>Ordered List</h2>
<ol>
  <li>Apples</li>
  <li>Berries</li>
  <li>Currants</li>
</ol>

<h2>Unordered List</h2>
<ul>
  <li>Carrots</li>
  <li>Celery</li>
  <li>Onions</li>
</ul>
```

It looks like this if you open the file in a browser.

Ordered List

1. Apples
2. Berries
3. Currants

Unordered List

- Carrots
- Celery
- Onions

List examples

We covered some basics here for HTML. There is a lot more

to learn. Of course, depending on your work this may be all you need. My development work has required me to use HTML periodically. Although, I am no expert. Play around with these and you will learn it well.

2

Important HTML5 Changes that Scream Out for Use

Photo by Jackson Sophat on Unsplash

HTML is like everything else. There are different versions we can use. HTML5 is a current version that has new features. Let's go through some of the changes and additions.

What is different?

Work has been done to remove the overlap between HTML, CSS, and JavaScript. Improvements have also been made to increase the readability of the code. Cross-browser consistency and responsiveness have been enhanced too. Finally, support of multimedia without plugins is another major change.

New Elements

In HTML5 there are new elements. The section tag was added to help organize the document.

```
<section>
<h2>Heading</h2>
<p>Lorem ipsum dolor sit amet, consectetur adipiscing
elit, sed do eiusmod tempor incididunt ut labore et
dolore magna aliqua. Ut enim ad minim veniam, quis
nostrud exercitation ullamco laboris nisi ut aliquip
ex ea commodo consequat. Duis aute irure dolor in
reprehenderit in voluptate velit esse cillum dolore
eu fugiat nulla pariatur. Excepteur sint occaecat
cupidatat non proident, sunt in culpa qui officia
deserunt mollit anim id est laborum.</p>
</section>
```

Similar to this tag we can also use header and footer tags. They are effectively organizing large chunks of HTML to make them more readable.

Form

To enable easier form creation HTML5 has added a few things.
Let's show the datetime-local input form element.

```
<input type="datetime-local">
```

If we run this in the browser we see this.

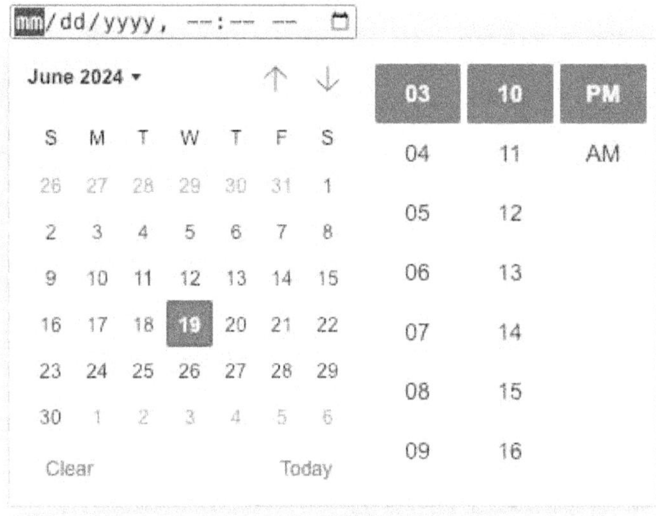

DateTime-Local example

That is nice compared to what we used to have to do for something like this.

Graphics

We can also add SVG or Scalable Vector Graphics in HTML5. Here is a simple example.

```
<svg width="100" height="100">
  <circle cx="50" cy="50" r="40" stroke="blue"
  stroke-width="4" fill="red" />
</svg>
```

If we run that in the browser you will see something like this.

SVG example

Not that impressive but it could be useful in some situations.

Offline

HTML5 enables offline work by storing local copies. So your browser will download the HTML, CSS, and JavaScript needed. This will allow you to work some without an internet connection.

HTML5 is a group of changes that enable better use of the web. From new elements and graphics, it helps the web take a step forward. Along with this, it makes the web more accessible. It is giving more and more people the ability to collaborate.

3

Practical HTML Tables, Divs, And Spans Make You Better

Photo by Alvin Engler on Unsplash

As I have worked with front-end technologies I see the approved way of working change. Web design norms come and go. HTML enables us various ways to create an interface.

Table

The HTML table is often derided but it can work. Early in my career tables were the way to go. Here is an example we can show the basic syntax.

```
<!DOCTYPE html>
<html>
    <style>
        table, th, td {
          border:1px solid black;
        }
        </style>
<body>

<table>
  <tr>
    <th>Company</th>
    <th>State</th>
    <th>Employees</th>
  </tr>
  <tr>
    <td>Balloons Inc.</td>
    <td>Ohio</td>
    <td>250</td>
  </tr>
  <tr>
    <td>Cement Co.</td>
    <td>Arizona</td>
    <td>4510</td>
  </tr>
</table>
```

```
</body>
</html>
```

Running this code gives us a simple table to display our data. Plan to not be amazed!

Company	State	Employees
Balloons Inc.	Ohio	250
Cement Co.	Arizona	4510

HTML Table Example

This simple example gives you an idea of how to use tables. There is a lot more we can do with them depending on your requirements.

Div

The div element is short for division. It creates a **block-level** section of HTML. We can style the div with CSS and manipulate it with JavaScript.

```
<!DOCTYPE html>
<html>
<head>
<style>
.exampleDiv {
  background-color: lightblue;
}
</style>
</head>
<body>

<h1>Let's talk about div elements!</h1>

<div class="exampleDiv">
  <h2>h2 in a div element</h2>
  <p>Text in a div element.</p>
</div>

<p>We have broken out of the div.</p>

</body>
</html>
```

We have an example that has the div in light blue. That way you can see where the div starts and stops.

Let's talk about div elements!

h2 in a div element

Text in a div element.

We have broken out of the div.

Div element example

In the picture, you can see the boundaries of the div and the rest of the page. If we applied styling it would only be within the div element.

Span

A span is an **inline container** we can add to an HTML document. Where a div is block-level and the span is inline. These are differences you may want to remember.

```
<!DOCTYPE html>
<html>
<body>

<h1>HTML Span element</h1>
```

```
<p>The fire truck is <span
style="color:red;font-weight:bold">red</span>.</p>
<p>The tree is <span
style="color:green;font-weight:bold">green</span>.</p>

</body>
</html>
```

Here we have two span elements used. We apply the styling here to change the color and put the font in bold.

HTML Span element

The fire truck is red.

The tree is green.

HTML Span example

We can see that the code does here. The next time you need a container for your HTML you can explore all three. The table, div, and span each have their pros and cons. Try out a simple example first to see what fits the bill correctly.

II

CSS

CSS is quite helpful in making websites more appealing. I have overlooked this for too long. I review some basics and then cover the box model. Finally, we cover CSS3.

4

The Truth About CSS Will Make You Something

Photo by Marcus Ganahl on Unsplash

Have you ever seen a website that looked weird? Do the fonts need to be corrected? This is when the CSS didn't load. It essentially makes the web look nice. I am not a font person but I understand the need for style.

CSS

CSS or Cascading Style Sheets apply the styling to websites. From text size and fonts, it can bring a touch of class to things.

```
<!DOCTYPE html>
<html>
<head>
<style>
body {
   background-color: lightpink;
}

h1 {
   color: white;
   text-align: center;
}

p {
   font-family: verdana;
   font-size: 20px;
}
</style>
</head>
<body>

<h1>H1 Heading(with center align)</h1>
<p>Paragraph(font size 20px and font verdana.</p>

</body>
</html>
```

Here is a simple HTML file with styling added. In this, we apply a background color to the body of the HTML. Then to the H1 heading we change the color and center the text. For the paragraph, we change the font and size. It looks like this.

HTML with Internal CSS Example

While HTML was just meant for text CSS was created to add style. If you are old enough to remember the initial web you are thankful! Things have come a long way.

Ways to Include

We showed you an example of an internal CSS above. The style tag is added in the HTML. We could also create an external document to put our CSS in.

```
<!DOCTYPE html>
<html>
<head>
<link rel="stylesheet" href="external-style.css">
</head>
<body>

<h1>We are using a CSS from another file.</h1>
<p>Aren't you impressed!</p>
```

```
</body>
</html>
```

This is our HTML file. Next, we can show you the code for the external CSS file.

```
body {
  background-color: lightblue;
}

h1 {
  color: navy;
  margin-left: 20px;
}
```

This works nicely as you can see below.

We are using a CSS from another file.

Aren't you impressed!

HTML with External CSS Example

With this example, you have two files. In a small example like this, it seems like overload. This is quite helpful in larger pages or if you have multiple pages. Then you can create one CSS file and include it in other HTML documents.

The last type is inline. See how the styling is in line here:

```html
<!DOCTYPE html>
<html>
  <head>
    <title>Inline CSS</title>
  </head>
  <body>
    <p style="color:rgb(149, 0, 255);font-size:46px;">
      I'm a big, purple, <strong>Proud UNI
      Panther</strong>!
    </p>
  </body>
</html>
```

This is mixing the CSS and HTML. For a beginner, this could be not very clear. Here is what it looks like.

I'm a big, purple, **Proud UNI Panther!**

HTML with Inline CSS Example

So when you add CSS to your HTML you have options on how to do it. As we discussed each way has its pros and cons. Depending on the size of your project and the team you are working with.

5

Wondrous CSS Box Model Made Instructive

Photo by Kelli McClintock on Unsplash

At first, CSS seemed like a black art for magicians only. Then as

I began to learn more it began to make sense. The box model is used to describe the design and layout of elements.

CSS Box Model

Each element has a box around it. Sometimes you can see it, other times it seems to disappear.
    Content — what is in the box, text, or image
    Padding — the area around the content, is transparent
    Border- goes around the padding and content
    Margin-the area outside of the border, it is also transparent
    Here is an example.

```
<!DOCTYPE html>
<html>
<head>
<style>
div {
   background-color: lightgrey;
   width: 300px;
   border: 10px solid red;
   padding: 25px;
   margin: 20px;
}
</style>
</head>
<body>

<h2>CSS Box Model</h2>

<p>A box around each component.</p>

<div>The content.<br>
25px padding<br>
```

```
20px margin<br>
10px red border.</div>

</body>
</html>
```

It looks like this.

CSS Box Model

A box around each component.

The content.
25px padding
20px margin
10px red border.

CSS Box Model Example

Size Math

To make the box the correct size we need to do some math. I know you weren't expecting that. It's easy so you won't be confused.

```
<!DOCTYPE html>
<html>
<head>
<style>
div {
   width: 300px;
   height: 65px;
   padding: 10px;
   border: 5px solid gray;
   margin: 0;
}
</style>
</head>
<body>

<h2>CSS Box Model Math</h2>

<div>This box is 300px wide and 50 px high. The
padding is 10px per side so 20px total. Then the
border 5px per side so 10px total. The total width of
this element is also 330px.</div>

</body>
</html>
```

When we run this code you will see the following.

CSS Box Model Math

This box is 300px wide and 50 px high. The padding is 10px per side so 20px total. Then the border 5px per side so 10px total. The total width of this element is also 330px.

CSS Box Model Math Example

We must add the content, padding, and border to get the total width. After I learned this CSS made more sense. Before I would start changing things trying to make it look right.

6

How To Make CSS3 Scream Simplified

Photo by KOBU Agency on Unsplash

As the web has changed so has the technology that supports it. CSS3 is one of these examples. CSS was originally released in

1996. A few years later CSS3 was released in 2005.

Benefits

One of the main benefits of CSS3 is responsive web design. It replaces clunky sites with more streamlined performance. There are new advanced animations and opacity features in CSS3.

Another benefit is the ability to break pages into modules. Media queries are also a new thing in CSS3. Plus we can now apply gradients and rounded corners as well.

Example

Let's look at an example of linear gradients.

```
<!DOCTYPE html>
<html lang="en">
<head>
<meta charset="utf-8">
<title>CSS Example of Linear Gradients from Top to
Bottom</title>
<style>
  .gradient {
  width: 400px;
  height: 300px;
  /* Fallback for browsers that don't support
  gradients */
  background: red;
  /* For Safari 5.1 to 6.0 */
  background: -webkit-linear-gradient(red, yellow);
  /* For Internet Explorer 10 */
  background: -ms-linear-gradient(red, yellow);
  /* Standard syntax */
  background: linear-gradient(red, yellow);
```

```
    }
    </style>
    </head>
    <body>
        <div class="gradient"></div>
    </body>
    </html>
```

When we look at this in the browser.

CSS3 Linear Gradient Example

What else can CSS3 do?

Box Shadow

It can also allow you to create a box shadow. Let's take a look.

```html
<!DOCTYPE html>
<html lang="en">
<head>
<meta charset="utf-8">
<title>Example of CSS3 Box Shadow Effect</title>
<style>
    .box{
  width: 200px;
  height: 150px;
  background: #ccc;
  box-shadow: 5px 5px 10px #999;
  }
</style>
</head>
<body>
    <div class="box"></div>
</body>
</html>
```

Open that in your browser and you should see something like this.

CSS3 Box Shadow Example

CSS3 has brought some major updates to CSS. As the web evolves there will be new updates. As a person who loves learning it is exciting to see the changes in the web. It is becoming easier to use and more robust.

III

JavaScript

In part three, we start with the basics of JavaScript. We code some fundamental aspects to help you understand how to get around.

7

JavaScript A Useful Tool For Tired Minds

I have a confession. JavaScript and I started badly. My first foray was for form validation. I would cuss about its existence.

As luck would have after being reintroduced to it I began to respect it. Over the years it has grown into a powerful language.

JavaScript

With its humble beginnings, JavaScript has evolved into a modern programming language. From the browser to the server it can handle almost everything. Node.js gives it a powerful framework on the server side.

Mozilla created it and here is how they define it. "JavaScript is a lightweight interpreted programming language with first-class functions." That is a mouthful!

Code

Let's look at some basic code. It is an HTML file displaying some JavaScript. Save this code to your local machine.

```
<!DOCTYPE html>

<head>
    <title>JavaScript example code</title>
    <style>

    </style>
</head>
<body>
    <script>
    alert("JavaScript is working!")
    </script>
    <h1>Test 1</h1>
    <h2>Test 2</h2>
    Regular text
</body>
```

When we run this we will see this.

JavaScript alert message

Once you click ok you will see this.

Test 1

Test 2

Regular text

HTML Screen-shot

Statement

The statement is the basic instruction for JavaScript. We can create some variables and then assign them values.

```
let a, b, c;       // Statement creating three variables
a = 2;             // Statement assign the value of 2 to
variable a
b = 3;             // Statement assign the value of 3 to
variable b
c = a + b;         // Statement assign a plus b to c
```

The **semicolon** is at the end of the statement. However, we could put multiple statements together.

```
a = 2; b = 3;
```

This isn't as readable so most programmers prefer not to. So just because you can do something doesn't mean you should.

Functions

When we want to perform a task we can create a function. If we need to sum two numbers we could do this in code or create a function.

```
// Add two numbers
num3 = num1 + num2;

// Function to sum two numbers
function sumTwoNumbers(num1, num2) {
   return num1 + num2;
}
```

In this example, we perform the same code one in a function and one not. Using a function has value. We can call it repeatedly. Also, we could easily add some error checking too.

```javascript
// Function to sum two numbers
function sumTwoNumbers(num1, num2) {
  return num1 + num2;
}

let sum = sumTwoNumbers(6,4);
```

We can do it like this example if you want to call the function. Here we pass in two numbers. These numbers could be replaced with variables as well.

In closing, we have touched on why we would use JavaScript. Then we started to code. Using statements and functions we began to see what is under the hood. Try it out for yourself! You won't regret it.

8

Look I found these astounding benefits of JavaScript variables and values

Photo by Khashayar Kouchpeydeh on Unsplash

Some people find differences easily. Their eye can see the one thing out of place. Others look for commonalities.

I find myself in the latter camp. Especially, as I look at

programming languages. JavaScript is quite similar to other languages. Let's focus on values and variables.

Values

The data we keep track of is our value. That could be some words or numbers. Perhaps even some special characters for the computer to process.

Variables

We give the data a name or a handle if you will. This allows us to reference it elsewhere.

```
let tomsJavaScriptVariable = "stuff";
```

This code example has a value, "stuff", and a variable name, **tomsJavaScriptVariable**. A lot happened here so let me explain it.

Declare

First thing we must declare a variable. This can be done by the following.

```
let declareVariable; // just declaring
```

The **let** keyword followed by the name declares the variable. Note our previous example set the value. This one does not.

Initialize

When we give it a value we are initializing the variable. So we can use our **declareVariable** here and initialize it too.

```
declareVariable = 123; // initialize variable
```

As you look through the examples you see that my first example did all this at once. So you can declare and initialize on separate lines or all at once. This can be personal preference. It can aid in the readability of separating them.

Naming

As you name your variables you have a few rules to learn in JavaScript. The length can be as short as one character. There is no upper limit. The first character is limited to letters, underscore(_), and dollar sign($). Numbers are not allowed for the first character.

```
let a; // letter
let areallylongnameforavariablethatyouwontwanttoread;
// long but legal
let _var; // underscore first
let $sal; // dollar sign first
let 4num; // illegal - won't work!
```

The other characters in the name can be letters, numbers, and characters. Also, the case can be mixed too.

```
let aMixtureOfUpperCaseAndLowerCase;
let a123$;
let _jsfgsiu$234432;
```

JavaScript gives you a lot of options to name your variables. Your fellow developers would appreciate meaningful names. I like to make wisecracks, but your code is not a good place to try this.

Const

If you have a variable you don't want to change you can use the const keyword to declare it. This is in place of the let keyword.

```
const pi = 3.14; // not able to change
let exhangeRate = 3.4; // able to change
```

Just make sure you think this through. Use the const keyword wisely. If you get crazy with it you will have issues.

let vs var

Variables can be declared with the var keyword too. Using the var keyword declares the variable in the whole function. While let is only for the block it is defined.

```
function varScoping() {
  var x = 1;

  if (true) {
    var x = 2;
    console.log(x); // will print 2
```

```
    }

    console.log(x); // will print 2
  }

function letScoping() {
  let x = 1;

  if (true) {
    let x = 2;
    console.log(x); // will print 2
  }

  console.log(x); // will print 1
}
```

This article shares more about these two options. It cannot be very clear to a newbie. Overall use let unless you need var. The global nature of var can cause some side effects.

These are the foundations of understanding JavaScript. Variables and values give us something to work with as we progress. We learned how to declare and initialize the variables. Plus we covered naming and different keywords to use.

9

First easy JavaScript function basics that are the most fascinating

Photo by Stanley Dai on Unsplash

Functions are the powerhouse in JavaScript. This is where the work happens. Do we need to calculate the space of a floor? This calls for a function.

```
function calculateFlooring(length, width) {
   return length * width;
}
```

This function will calculate the flooring we need if we remodel the kitchen. So why do we need functions?

Benefits

Think of a function as a container for your code. Similar to a code block but, we can call this function repeatedly. This will facilitate reusable code.

In our prior example, you could copy the statement. Of course, if we wanted to change that we needed to search for that code and change all the occurrences.

Example

In our first function example, we calculated the flooring. Let's step back and make it even easier. We can print something on the screen.

```
function greetTom() {
   alert("Hello Tom!");
}
```

Of course, you can put your name in place of mine. If you want to keep the tradition, you can replace it with "Hello World". Have you wondered why that is the tradition, look here.

Calling

The code may look nice but nothing happens if you don't call it. How do you do that? I am glad you asked. Here is an example.

```
function greetTom() {
  alert("Hello Tom!");
}


greetTom();
// do other things...
```

That call is easy as it takes no arguments. In our first function, we had two arguments we needed. Let's try that next.

Passing arguments

In our first example, we started with a function to calculate flooring. It took two arguments.

```
function calculateFlooring(length, width) {
  return length * width;
}


calculateFlooring(12,10);
```

We can pass in the two numbers to get the flooring needed. In this example, we hard-code the value. You won't do that often or ever.

```
function calculateFlooring(length, width) {
  return length * width;
}


calculateFlooring(length,width);
```

As you see here, we have the two arguments as variables. The names are the same as the function but don't have to be.

Returning data

It is helpful when we return the calculation. If we don't the function is not as useful as it could be. We just need to use the return. We did this in our calculate flooring function. Although we need to assign this or print it out.

```
function calculateFlooring(length, width) {
  return length * width;
}

let totalFlooring = 0;
totalFlooring = calculateFlooring(length,width);
```

Now we can use this value later in the application. The prior examples didn't use the value returned. This is always an option if you don't need it later on.

Functions can do a lot for us. They provide us with a container for our code. Then we can call them and pass parameters. Along with that, they can return the data. If you need more information here is some further reading.

10

Avoid painful mistakes with these Simplistic JavaScript Conditionals

Photo by Artur Aldyrkhanov on Unsplash

Applications help us make decisions. A basic decision is an if condition. For example, if the pizza delivery driver arrives open the door. JavaScript like other languages has many conditionals like Java.

if

An if statement starts with a condition. If it is true the statement following will happen.

```
if(pizzaArrives) {
   openTheDoor();
}
```

So if pizzaArrives is true we call the function openTheDoor. I added the braces after the if statement. This is optional but helps readability. Omitting the braces can cause you to miss bugs. So please include them!

if/else

There are times when you have two different courses of action. We can add the else statement along with the if. Say you are cooking some hamburgers.

```
if(sideCooked) {
   flipBurger();
} else {
   keepCooking();
}
```

This check can run the cooking robot at your favorite house of burgers. It might need some more code though.

If you need to check two conditions you can have an if else if too.

```
if(sideCooked) {
  flipBurger();
} else if(otherSideCooked) {
  removeFromGrill();
} else {
  keepCooking();
}
```

This gives us the option to check additional values. If you need more checks a switch statement may work better. More on that later.

Conditional Operators

The operators we use for if statements must resolve to true or false. There are quite a few options for you to use here. Speaking from experience you need to test things out and get the right one.

```
if(9>5) { alert("Greater than"); }// greater than
if(5<8) { alert("Less than"); } // less than
if(9>=6) { alert("Greater than equal to"); } //
greater than equal to
if(4<=6) { alert("Less than equal to"); } // less
than equal to
if(4!=6) { alert("Not equal to"); } // not equal to
```

There are also two logical operators. The Logical And(&&) and the Logical Or(||). They are used a lot but don't be intimidated.

```
const value1 = 4;
const value2= -3;

console.log(value1 > 0 && value2 > 0); // Expected
output: false
console.log(value1 > 0 || value2 > 0); // Expected
output: true
```

The Logical And must have both values true to resolve as true. The Logical Or needs one to be true.

switch

Switch statements evaluate the expression to determine which statement to execute. Then it runs the code until reaching a break statement. Here is an example that tells us the price of the shoes you want.

```
const shoes = 'Reebok';
switch (shoes) {
  case 'Nike':
    console.log('Nike shoes are $200.');
    break;
  case 'Adidas':
  case 'Reebok':
    console.log('Adidas and Reebok are $100 a pair.');
    // Expected output: "Adidas and Reebok are $100 a
    pair."
    break;
  default:
```

```javascript
    console.log(`Sorry, we don't carry ${shoes}.`);
  }
```

This code should print "Adidas and Reebok are $100 a pair." to the console. Switch statements can be tricky if you don't add the break statement.

```javascript
const shoes = 'Nike';
switch (shoes) {
  case 'Nike':
    console.log('Nike shoes are $200.');
  case 'Adidas':
  case 'Reebok':
    console.log('Adidas and Reebok are $100 a pair.');
    break;
  default:
    console.log(`Sorry, we don't carry ${shoes}.`);
}
```

In this example, we removed the break from the Nike statement. Do you know what happens here? It will print 'Nike shoes are $200.' and then 'Adidas and Reebok are $100 a pair.' This type of bug is common for beginner programmers. Don't feel bad. You are now part of the club!

Conditionals are fundamental to JavaScript. Similar to other languages it allows us to provide solutions quickly. The if/else and switch are easy to use.

11

JavaScript has Sizable loops that will explode your mind

Photo by Kier in Sight Archives on Unsplash

As a kid, we planted a windbreak on our farm. A line of trees that needed watering a few times a week. Turn on the hose water the first tree and count to ten. Move to the second tree and repeat.

Similar to life our computer programs must repeat things. That's where loops come in handy. For loops are quite common so let's start there.

for

If we have an array of books and we would like to print them out. We could use the following loop.

```javascript
for (let i = 0; i < books.length; i++) {
  text += books[i] + "<br>";
}
```

The for loop has three basic parts. Start, Condition, and Step.

start

This is the part where we set up the loop variable. In our example that is **i**. Usually, we initialize to zero. Although, you can set it to say 10 and then count down too.

condition

Next is the condition where check to see if we need to run this loop again. Our example checks if we still have more books to loop through. If we are done we stop.

step

The last part is the step. This tells us what happens after each iteration. Our example uses the increment operator(++). This is the normal step but we can do other things for special cases.

while

If my dog Baxter wants to eat I want to create a loop that feeds him while he is hungry. The while loop can do this. Here is an example.

```
let baxterHungry = true;

while (baxterHungry) {
    console.log(feedBaxter);
    checKBaxter();
}
```

We set the variable to true. Then we feed the dog until it becomes false. The while loop evaluates the condition we give it. It needs to resolve to be true or false.

If it is true the code inside the loop executes. We evaluate the condition again. Once the condition becomes false the loop stops.

do-while

The for and while loops check the condition then run the code statements. The do-while is different in that it runs the code and then checks your condition. It is less common but useful in special situations.

```javascript
let donutsEaten = 0;
do {
   console.log("Donuts eaten " + donutsEaten);
   donutsEaten++;
} while (donutsEaten < 5)
console.log("I'm full of Donuts!");
```

The do while runs until the condition is false—Opposite of the two other types of loops we have discussed. The output would look like this.

```
Donuts eaten 0
Donuts eaten 1
Donuts eaten 2
Donuts eaten 3
Donuts eaten 4
I'm full of Donuts!
```

When you need to loop through code JavaScript has a few options for you. Like other programming languages, it has the for, while, and do-while loops. Just make sure it fits your needs.

12

Surprisingly Improved JavaScript Variable Scope You Need

Photo by Markus Spiske on Unsplash

My wife changes topics quickly. I joke with her that she needs turn signals. That way I can keep up with the shifting focus. She is talking about dinner, and then we shift to our next vacation.

Scope

Our code has a similar concept with scope. Variables can come in and out of scope quickly. As developers, we must keep this concept front and center.

In JavaScript, they have a few different types of scope. We can use them accordingly. If you have done other coding you have encountered similar concepts.

Global

Global scope items are visible everywhere. In our example, we create a visible variable in the function and outside.

```
let myGlobalVariable = "TheBigGlobalVariable";

function logOutGlobalVariable() {
    console.log(myGlobalVariable);
}

logOutGlobalVariable();
```

I bet you are wondering, what if I add a variable in the function? This leads us to the local scope example.

Local

Local variables are visible only in the function. Here is an example to try this out.

```
let myGlobalVariable = "TheBigGlobalVariable";

function logOutGlobalVariable() {
    console.log(myGlobalVariable);
    let localVariable = "TheLocalOne";
    console.log(localVariable);
}

logOutGlobalVariable();

console.log(localVariable);
```

If we run this we will get an error on the last line.

```
console.log(localVariable);
          ^

ReferenceError: localVariable is not defined
```

So you can see what happens when you mistakenly place a variable in the wrong spot.

Block

Where local scope is within the function, block scope is within the braces. Sometimes you create braces to identify some code. Let's take a look to show you what I mean.

```
console.log("here");
{
  let blockScopeVariable = 0;
  console.log(blockScopeVariable);
}
// we can't reference blockScopeVariable here
console.log(blockScopeVariable); // won't work
```

As you can see we create a block scope variable within the braces. Then outside of that, it won't be able to be referenced.

Gotchas

The scope can be confusing and lead to some errors. As you get more experience with JavaScript, you can spot them early on. For instance, if we look at this code snippet:

```
const colors = ['red', 'blue', 'white'];

for (let i = 0, var l = colors.length; i < l; i++) {
  console.log(colors[i]); // 'red', 'blue', 'white'
}
console.log(l); // ???
console.log(i); // ???
```

The variables i and l will get reference errors. They are out of scope similar to our previous examples. Dmitri Pavlutin explains this more in-depth here. He also covers a few more common mistakes we may make in coding.

JavaScript scope has a few basic principles you need to remember. Global scope is visible everywhere. Local and Block scope are more focused. Overall you should use the latter and avoid the former. Keep on coding!

Exploit JavaScript Closures More and Don't Panic

Photo by Cristina Gottardi on Unsplash

Having dipped into JavaScript occasionally over my development career Closures have been something I didn't encounter much. They have some great value.

Closures

How can we define closures? Well, this article defines it like this. "Closure in JavaScript is a form of **lexical scoping** used to preserve variables from the outer scope of a function in the inner scope of a function."

```
function outerFunction() {
  var x = 10;
  function innerFunction() {
    return x;
  }
  return innerFunction;
}


var inner = outerFunction();
console.log(inner());
```

Here is an example of a closure. The outer function outer-Function() creates a variable x and a function innerFunction(). The inner function innerFunction() returns the value of the variable x. The outer function then returns the inner function innerFunction().

Next inner function innerFunction() is then assigned to the variable inner. When the variable inner is called, it returns the value of the variable x, even though the outer function outerFunction() has already returned.

In a moment we can cover lexical scoping. First, let's understand why we need them. Plus some disadvantages too.

Pros and Cons

Closures can help hide the encapsulation details. Like Java's private variables and functions, this allows us to control access. The downside of this is closures take up more memory. These items can not be garbage collected. Lastly, it can slow down execution. Deepak Mankotia explores this more in-depth.

Lexical Scoping

The term lexical scoping refers to where the variable is defined. Along with that where it can be referenced or not.

```
let x = 10
let myFunc = function (){
let y = 20;
    console.log("x and y is accessible (outer):", x,
    y);
    let insideFunc= function (){
        let z = 30;
        console.log("x and y and z is accessible
        (inner):", x, y, z);
    }
    insideFunc();
    return;
}
 myFunc();
 console.log("only x is accessible (global):", a);
```

In this example, insideFunc is defined within the myFunc. In this case, myFunc is its parent. That of the parent function lexically binds the child function. JavaScript Closures are a form of Lexical Scoping.

JavaScript Closures are powerful tools. They have some distinct values. It allows you to encapsulate details but, it can slow down your execution time. Consider whether the risks and rewards work for your application.

For more information here is a deep dive on Closures.

About the Author

Tom Henricksen is a problem-solving technology professional. He is a speaker and writer at Code is Easy. Starting from a developer he has worked as a Project Manager, Technical Lead, Scrum Master, and Manager of Software Development.

Tom has helped organizations with agile transformations. He has also coached and trained teams and individuals.

Tom has been an entrepreneur as well. He speaks and writes with a focus on technology roles. Tom was the founder of the Agile Online Summit and DevOps Online Summit where he led a strong online community of over 5,000 people.

Tom has learned how to solve challenging issues in technology and lead technical teams. He can help you develop those skills too!

You can connect with me on:

- http://codeiseasy.co
- https://twitter.com/TomHenricksen
- https://www.linkedin.com/in/tomhenricksen

Subscribe to my newsletter:

- https://t.co/NkolrQgXHM